The PMP Translator

Kate Breitfeller

Jason Breitfeller, MBA, PMP

ISBN:
978-1717396938

DEDICATION

To all of the hardworking people trying to keep their projects on time, on schedule, and on budget.

CONTENTS

INTRODUCTION

Let's be honest....anytime you start something new there is a learning curve that you will need to overcome. How steep and how fast you navigate that curve will depend on your experience! Studying for and passing the PMP® exam is no exception. Our goal in creating the PMP Translator, is to help both the long-time PMP and the future PMP understand and digest the terms in the Project Management Body of Knowledge Version 6 (PMBOK6®). The Translator identifies and prioritizes these essential terms in an efficient, effective way to showcase what's important and how the fancy vocabulary ties back to real world issues.

In a lot of ways, the terms that the Project Management Institute (PMI®) uses are a foreign language! You can have tons of management experience and the best education, but that doesn't mean that you will automatically speak the language that PMI has defined. Some of the definitions are extremely confusing and, by the time you've read it three times, you still aren't exactly sure what they mean. Not to mention the fact that the sheer number of terms that PMI includes in the PMBOK can be overwhelming! In order to pass the test and succeed, you need to not only memorize over 1,000 terms but understand where they fit into each of the process groups!

You may already be familiar with some of these terms and some you may know by a different name. However, to pass the PMP exam you have to know PMI's *specific* definition! After 20 years of working with the materials in the PMBOK Guide, we've accepted that using this new "language" is a part of what makes it special to be a PMP. It also bridges the communication gap between companies across different industries because everyone has a common lexicon.

The goal of this book is *NOT* to teach you every term!!! We counted...no really...we counted the terms in the PMBOK6 and, after analysis, what we discovered was eye opening! Of the 146 unique Inputs, Tools, and Outputs, 32 of the unique terms appear 80% of the time.

We have broken it down into the top 20 terms and THOSE are the ones you need to focus on. For example, Expert Judgment appears 35 times in PMBOK6 Guide Processes. You only need to learn it once!

When you really think about it, Project Management is just common sense written down.....and that's the approach we took with the PMP Translator. Using the premise of a home improvement project, we introduce and explain all 20 essential terms. The characters, Sally and Ben, are representative of the majority of PMs in the work force that are trying, day after day, to do the right thing. For the purpose of learning the most frequently used terms the story is not presented in perfect chronological order but in the order of frequency that they appear in the PMBOK6.

By no means is this guide meant to be an exhaustive source for understanding and passing the PMP exam! There are a ton of great sources already available! This book is intended to be used as a tool. One that will enhance your overall approach to studying for the PMP exam by focusing your efforts and allowing you to get the most out of your study time. The PMP Translator explains in everyday language what the most common terms mean and how they work, through a simple, real-life scenario that everyone can understand!

Happy Reading and Good Luck!

INPUTS

Organizational Process Assets (OPA)

Used 47 times!

Definition: **The plans, processes, policies, procedures, and knowledge bases specific to and used by the performing organization. These assets influence the management of the project.**

When/Where: **Used in all processes EXCEPT: Validate Scope, Monitor Risks**

"I need to be sure I send Rick a request for quote about the bathroom today," Sally said, as she rinsed the coffee mugs. She made a face. "I guess I need to list out everything we are looking for, time frame and budget etc."

"You don't need to start from scratch," Ben reminded her. "You probably still have the email you sent him when you wanted a proposal to do the floors. **(Process, Policy, Procedure)** Why don't you start with that and just modify it to fit this project? There will be a lot of similarities between the two projects. He's going to have to do the demolition and order the supplies just like before, and that will already be in there. **(Template)** You'll save yourself a lot of time and hassle that way." As Ben picked up his wallet and keys, he added, "In fact, you might even tell Rick that he could use the same basic schedule as before. **(Template)** We added milestones as we went along with the floors. No reason to think it won't be the same this time." Smirking, he added "Something always pops up." **(Lessons Learned)**

Sally threw the dish towel at him. "You know you like having the electrical outlets in the floor even if it did push the schedule and budget out a bit!"

Ben grinned. "True, and I'm sure whatever you add on this time will be just as useful dear." He winked at her, but then sobered for a moment. "Hey, since there is going to be tile work done again, let's make sure Rick doesn't hire that tile installer he started with on the floors. I don't think that man even *owned* a level!" **(Lesson Learned)**

“Good point!!” Sally made a note on her note pad. “I’m just going to use Quicken again to track the payments. **(Organizational Knowledge Base)** It’s easier than trying to remember in my head when I need to have the funds available.”

Ben leaned over to give his wife a kiss goodbye. “Excellent! Looking forward to getting the project done!”

Project Management Plan (PMP)

Used 47 times as Input, 1 time as Output!

<u>Definition:</u> **The document that describes how the project will be executed, monitored and controlled, and closed.**

<u>When/Where:</u> **Used in all processes *EXCEPT* Develop Project Charter, Develop Project Management Plan; OUTPUT: *Develop Project Management Plan***

"Hey, Angela!" Sally said as she slid into the seat across from her friend. "Is this coffee for me?" She put her purse in the seat next to her and a giant binder on the low table between them.

"What the heck is that?" Her friend laughed.

Sally grimaced as she gestured to it. "That's my project binder for the bathroom. **(Project Management Plan)** I keep it with me just in case I need to check something! It's turned out to be a little more complicated than I had planned. But, fortunately, Ben is a real stickler for making sure everything is where it needs to be, so we came up with this as a way to make sure everything was in one place." She laughed, "You'd be surprised how many times this baby has come in handy when Ben and I disagree on what we had originally planned to do! The binder is the Ref!"

Angela looked doubtful as she ran her finger over the colorful tabs sticking out the side. "What exactly do you have in there?"

"Oh! Everything!" Opening the binder, Sally flipped through the labeled dividers to show how it was organized. "I've got pictures of what I want to be included **(Scope Management Plan),** our timeline on when certain things are supposed to be done **(Schedule Management Plan),** how much and when money has to be spent **(Cost Management Plan),** all kinds of fun stuff like that." She laughed at her friend's bewildered expression.

"You realize that you sound like a total nerd right?"

"Oh yeah! Absolutely! But let me tell you, when you put it in writing, nobody can claim 'I don't remember agreeing to that'." Sally patted the binder affectionately. "This baby has all the proof! We even put in writing that we weren't going to let our respective parents know what we were doing, because *everybody* has an opinion on what we should do and how much we should spend! **(Stakeholder Engagement Plan)** It's easier to just let them be surprised when they come visit after it's all done."

"That's actually a really good idea!" Angela said. "Can I look?" She flipped to the green tab. "What is this?" she asked looking at a line graph.

"That's just a sanity check for us. In the beginning of the project, it always feels like money is pouring out but there's nothing to show for it. I mean, you can write a check for tile to be ordered but it's not fun 'til it's installed. This graph just reminds us that, even though we expect to spend $10,000 the first month—the down payment and supplies, the next $10,000 is paid out over the last two months of the project. **(Cost Baseline)**

The buzzing of Sally's phone distracted her from her friend's skeptical expression. Seeing Rick's name on the caller ID, she sighed.

"What is it?" Angela asked.

"It's Rick, our contractor. He's a really nice guy but one of the things we laid out in the beginning with him was that I couldn't do phone calls during the day. If he has a minor issue question, he could text it but that any major changes to the original plan need to be writing." She flipped to the orange tab and pointed to a typed paragraph. "I even put it in writing!" **(Communications Management Plan)**

"Does Ben go along with the whole...." Angela waved her hand at the binder.

"Of course! Once a week we go over the plan and check in with each other to make sure we are both on the same page. **(Additional Components)** I know we might seem extreme, but it really does make sure everything gets done and nothing gets overlooked! Do you want to see the section where we wrote out that we have to discuss any material change over $300?" **(Change Management Plan)**

"No, I'm ok......"

Project Documents

Used 43 times!

<u>Definition:</u> **Documents used to both streamline and successfully complete a project including project charter, project management plan, change requests, work performance reports, and change log.**

<u>When/Where:</u> **Used in all processes *EXCEPT*: Develop Project Charter, Develop Project Management Plan, Plan Scope Management, Plan Schedule Management, Define Activities, Plan Cost Management**

When Sally arrived home after work, she knew by the look on Rick's face that there was a problem.

"What's wrong?" she asked nervously. Rick made a face.

"We reached the point in demolition that I needed to shut the water off in the shower so that we could cap and move the pipes. As you know, your shut off is under the sink." He walked over and opened the cabinet. "Unfortunately, we discovered you've had a leak for quite some time down there. You can even see the mold."

Horrified, Sally ducked her head down to look. "Oh no!!"

"Because it's the shut off, you really need to have it fixed before we move on." He looked at her seriously. "This was not in my original quote for either the schedule or the budget...I know how important that is to you guys." Sally took a deep breath.

"No, it will be OK. I had some risk built in. I'll update it once we sign a change order. **(Risk Register)** I guess I really should have had you check out all the plumbing before we did a final quote." **(Lesson Learned)**

"It shouldn't be that bad. I'll write up a change order for you that you can use to update your budget and schedule. If you can get this cabinet cleared out tonight, I can probably get it done pretty fast." **(Update Activity List)**

Enterprise Environmental Factors (EEF)

Used 40 times!

Definition: **Conditions, not under the immediate control of the team, that influence, constrain, or direct the project, program, or portfolio.**

When/Where: **Used in all processes EXCEPT: Close Project or Phase, Validate Scope, Control Scope, Control Schedule, Control Costs, Manage Quality, Control Resources, Implement Risk Responses, Monitor Risks**

Two weeks before the project begins

"Are you excited to work with us again, Rick?" Sally joked. "We are so low maintenance!"

Rick laughed good-naturedly. "You guys aren't that bad! Everything is going to be fine and we are going to have another successful project!"

Sally smiled as she walked him to the door. "OK, just as a reminder since we are a gated community, you can't start work before 8 am." **(Enterprise Environmental Factors)**

"No problem, I'm used to HOA restrictions."

Project Charter

Used 14 times as Input, 1 time as Output!

Definition: **A document issued by the project initiator or sponsor that formally authorizes the existence of a project and provides the project manager with the authority to apply organizational resources to project activities.**

When/Where: **Develop project management, close project or phase, plan scope management, collect requirements, define scope, plan schedule management, plan cost management, plan quality management, plan resource management, plan communications management, plan risk management, plan procurement management, identify stakeholders, plan stakeholder engagement; OUTPUT:** ***Develop project charter***

August

"We have to get a new bathroom," Sally **(Project Initiator, Key Stakeholder)** told her husband, Ben, **(Key Stakeholder)** over coffee. "The shower tile is collapsing. We have to replace it before we get water damage."

Ben nodded. "We've put this off for a while but it's time to finally do something about it. Do you have a plan in mind?"

"Well, we obviously need a new shower and, as long as we are ripping it out, I'd like to expand it by 3 feet. Maybe some new countertops, too." **(High Level Requirement)** "Let me grab a piece of paper and we can write down what we need." Sally grabbed a notebook and began jotting down notes as they talked.

"Ok, what about the floor? Can we keep the tile or does that need to be replaced too?" **(Project Boundary)**

"No, the floor is fine. That can stay the same"

"Well, if we are going to lose the bathroom for a while, I've always wanted one of those Japanese toilets that is fully automated!" **(Deliverable)**

"If I'm getting the extended shower, it's only fair you should get something you want too," Sally said with a smile.

"We need to be sure it's done by the Super Bowl though, because my family is coming about that time and we will need both bathrooms in the house operational." Sally nodded.

"I agree. So, let's plan on 3 months and have a cushion of 3 additional months in case of contractor over runs." **(Overall Risk)**

"So, what do you think? About a week for the demo?" **(Milestone)**

"That sounds about right."

"Are you going to be able to do this on your own?" Ben asked. "My schedule has me traveling a lot over the next several months. I'm not sure how much help I'll be," he grinned. "That doesn't mean you should add a marble steam shower though!" **(Project Approval Requirements)**

"No problem! If something major comes up I'll check with you, but I can handle the contractor on this end. Do you want to use our home equity line of credit?" **(Prepared Financial Resources)**

"That's probably the best route. But, don't forget it only lets you use $10,000.00 a month so you'll need to figure out when to order supplies and when the contractor gets his payments. Are you going to use Rick **(Key Stakeholder)** again? He did a great job on the floors."

"Absolutely! He's reasonably priced and reliable. I'll give him a call."

Work Performance Data

Used 11 times, 1 time as an Output!

Definition: **The raw observations and measurements identified during activities being performed to carry out the project work.**

When/Where: **Validate Scope, Control Scope, Control Schedule, Control Costs, Control Quality, Control Resources, Monitor Communications, Monitor Risks, Control Procurements, Monitor Stakeholder Engagement; OUTPUT: *Direct and Manage Project Work***

Sally was exhausted by the time she got home and was not pleased to see Rick's truck still in the driveway. Putting down her bag she joined Rick in the bathroom, where he was just packing up his things.

"Hey Rick! How was today?" Rick looked up and smiled.

"It was really productive actually!" He gestured to the room. "The plumber got done at about 1 pm **(Actual Finish Statistic)**, so the tile guys were able to get started around 2 pm and work until 4 pm. **(Actual Statistics)** I thought the glass installers were going to come by to talk about the enclosure but they said they couldn't be here until 5:30 and that was too late." Rick trailed off seeing Sally's lack of enthusiasm.

"Well anyway, I guess, I better get going. I'm supposed to be at my son's school for a play tonight."

As Rick made his way to the front door he waved to Ben who was just coming in.

"Hi Honey!" Ben said, giving Sally a quick kiss. "How was your day?"

"Long and irritating." Sally groused. "The last thing I wanted when I got home, was to get a minute by minute recitation of the subcontractors' activities today! I felt like saying 'I don't care what each person is doing, I just want to know when it's going to be done!' " Ben grimaced.

"I guess that means I shouldn't ask how much we've spent so far, like I was planning to." Sally sighed.

"No, it's OK. We've spent about $10,340 so far." **(Actual Cost)**

"Is it safe to ask about the hole they knocked in the dry wall by the bedroom door?" Ben asked warily.

"Yes," Sally rolled her eyes. "Rick made sure it was fixed and we won't be billed. **(Defect Repair)** You make me sound like I'm a time bomb! I don't mind answering your questions!" Ben pinched his lips together to keep from smiling before wryly saying.

"You are totally correct. You have been the picture of patience."

TOOLS

Expert Judgment

Used 35 Times!

Definition: **Judgment provided based upon expertise in an application area, knowledge area, discipline, industry, etc., as appropriate for the activity being performed. Such expertise may be provided by any group or person with specialized education, knowledge, skill, experience, or training.**

When/Where: **Develop Project Charter, Develop Project Management Plan, Direct and Manage Project Work, Manage Project Knowledge, Monitor & Control Project Work, Perform Integrated Change Control, Close Project or Phase, Plan Scope Management, Collect Requirements, Define Scope, Create WBS, Plan Schedule Management, Define Activities, Estimate Activity Durations, Plan Cost Management, Estimate Costs, Determine Budget, Control Costs, Plan Quality Management, Plan Resource Management, Estimate Activity Resources, Plan Communications Management, Monitor Communications, Plan Risk Management, Identify Risks, Perform Qualitative Analysis, Perform Quantitative Analysis, Plan Risk Responses, Implement Risk Responses, Plan Procurement Management, Conduct Procurement, Control Procurement, Identify Stakeholders, Plan Stakeholder Engagement, Manage Stakeholder Engagement**

"You really think we should leave the on/off handle in line with the new shower head?" Sally was disappointed. She had seen a picture of a shower on the internet that had the on/off handle offset from the shower head so that the water could be turned on without getting into the shower.

Rick shrugged. "I just don't see the point. You'd still have to step into the shower to see if the water is the right temperature. If we offset it, I'm going to have to cut more holes in the wall."

"Would that affect the budget or schedule?"

"Not really. Just seems unnecessary." Sally wasn't convinced.

"OK, well, we aren't quite at the point where we *have* to make a decision so let me think about it."

The next day, Sally made a point to stop by her neighbor Rachel's house. Rachel had just had her bathroom redone and Sally knew that she was extremely happy about the result.

"Hey Rachel! This is going to sound like a really odd question but......could I see your new shower?"

"Sure, not a problem!" As they walked toward the Master Bathroom Sally said,

"I might be crazy but didn't you say that you had decided to offset the shower handle from the shower head?"

"Yeah, it's about a foot away. I love it because I can turn on the shower without getting wet." She gestured to the new shower.

"But what about knowing the temperature, wouldn't you still have to get wet?"

"I guess, but it's not an issue. Besides, if you are really worried about it you can get one of those new shower systems that have a temperature readout."

"My contractor thinks I shouldn't do it, that it's a waste. If you had to do it again, would you still design it the same?" **(Expert Judgment)**

"Definitely! It's one of my favorite features!"

Data Analysis

Used 32 Times!

Definition: **Techniques used to organize, assess, and evaluate data and information.**

When/Where: **Monitor and Control Project Work, Perform Integrated Change Control, Close Project or Phase, Plan Scope Management, Collect Requirements, Define Scope, Control Scope, Plan Schedule Management, Estimate Activity Duration, Develop Schedule, Control Schedule, Plan Cost Management, Estimate Costs, Determine Budget, Control Costs, Plan Quality Management, Manage Quality, Control Quality, Estimate Activity Resources, Control Resources, Plan Risk Management, Identify Risks, Perform Qualitative Analysis, Perform Quantitative Analysis, Plan Risk Responses, Monitor Risks, Plan Procurement Management, Conduct Procurements, Control Procurements, Identify Stakeholders, Plan Stakeholder Engagement, Monitor Stakeholder Engagement**

"OK, I've got some bad news." Sally sighed. When these are the first words out of your contractor's mouth, you know you aren't going to be happy with what comes next. Anticipating a difficult conversation with him she could feel her shoulders tighten. "The shower head with all the different nozzles you picked out is back ordered at least a month. There's no guarantee as to when it will arrive."

"Seriously!?" Sally was very disappointed. She had loved the design and the price was perfect. Maybe *too* perfect if everyone else had ordered it too!

"So, you need to decide if you want to stick with that shower head and miss your deadline or, if you want, to pick something else out." **(Alternatives Analysis)**

Rick pulled out his iPad and opened up an image of a different shower head. "This one is very similar to the original one and the vendor has it in stock. Unfortunately, it's about $50 more than you had originally budgeted." Sally frowned. Which was more important to her and Ben? To have a completely separate bathroom by the time their guests arrived or to spend more on this new shower head? **(Cost/Benefit Analysis)**

"Let's go ahead and order this new one. Even though it will cost a little more, there will still be time in the schedule if there are any problems with the install."

"Great! I'll take care of that right away."

"Actually, Rick, there is something else I wanted to talk to you about. Your first bill has come in at $10,300 and I don't understand why." It was Rick's turn to frown.

"Sally, you know that demolition took a lot longer than we had originally estimated! There was no way I could have known that there was a second subfloor underneath the shower!" **(Variance Analysis)**

"I remember, I just didn't realize it had affected the budget so much. OK, now I understand why the estimate changed."

The Next Month

"Rick, thanks for meeting with me this morning. I'm very happy with the work you are doing but now, for the second month in a row, the bill has come in over the $10,000 limit we had set." **(Trend)**

"I didn't anticipate having to order all of the materials so early in the project. Normally, I'm able to spread out the expenditures over a longer period, but many of the products you chose had a long lead time. So, I had to order them early!" Rick said annoyed.

"I'm not saying that you are wasting money. It's just that we have limits to our financial funding that are beyond our control. I can pay this bill but, if it happens again, I'm going to have to wait until the end of the contract to pay you for the overages."

Rick clearly did not like this solution but couldn't dispute the contract he had signed.

Meetings

Used 28 Times!

Definition: **Any time two or more people get together to exchange information.**

When/Where: **Develop Project Charter, Develop Project Management Plan, Direct and Manage Project Work, Monitor and Control Project Work, Perform Integrated Change Control, Close Project or Phase, Plan Scope Management, Plan Schedule Management, Define Activities, Estimate Activity Duration, Plan Cost Management, Plan Quality Management, Control Quality, Plan Resource Management, Estimate Activity Resources, Develop Team, Plan Communications Management, Manage Communications, Monitor Communications, Plan Risk Management, Identify Risks, Perform Qualitative Analysis, Monitor Risks, Plan Procurement Management, Identify Stakeholders, Plan Stakeholder Engagement, Manage Stakeholder Engagement, Monitor Stakeholder Engagement**

On Saturday morning, Ben and Sally were enjoying their coffee while Sally updated Ben on how the bathroom project was going. **(Status Meeting)**

"So, we had the leak under the sink which stinks, but the change order is signed and everything is fixed. Demolition took a little longer than expected because they found a second subfloor of all things under the shower!"

"When does he order the tile? I don't want us to get held up waiting on product to arrive."

"Already done!" Sally grinned.

"Great! Sounds like everything is going fairly smoothly, let's hope it continues!"

Interpersonal and Team Skills

Used 20 Times!

Definition: **Skills used to effectively lead and interact with team members and other stakeholders.**

When/Where: **Develop Project Charter, Develop Project Management Plan, Manage Project Knowledge, Collect Requirements, Define Scope, Acquire Resources, Develop Team, Manage Team, Control Resources, Plan Communications Management, Manage Communications, Identify Risks, Perform Qualitative Analysis, Perform Quantitative Analysis, Plan Risk Responses, Implement Risk Responses, Conduct Procurements, Manage Stakeholder Engagements, Monitor Stakeholder Engagements**

Sally was already at the kitchen table with her coffee when her husband Ben strode angrily into the room.

"Have you seen the shower? It looks terrible!"

"I haven't looked at it since they finished working yesterday. Is it bad?"

"Is it bad?! A first grader could do better! Haven't you been checking the work??" Ben's voice rose with frustration.

"I understand you are upset." Sally kept her voice calm. "What *exactly* do you not like? Is it the tile itself or the quality of the work?" **(Conflict Management)** Ben plopped down in his chair.

"The tile is fine, great actually. What you picked out looks fantastic. But whoever installed it made the grout lines huge. It ruins the look."

"I'll let Rick know. I don't think they've done so much that it can't be fixed." **(Facilitation)**

Later that day, Sally sent Rick an email requesting that he be available at 9 o'clock the next morning to discuss the tile installation. **(Meeting Management)**

Data Gathering

Used 13 Times!

Definition: **Techniques used to collect data and information from a variety of sources.**

When/Where: **Develop Project Charter, Develop Project Management, Collect Requirements, Plan Quality Management, Manage Quality, Control Quality, Identify Risks, Perform Qualitative Analysis, Perform Quantitative Analysis, Plan Risk Responses, Plan Procurement Management, Identify Stakeholders, Plan Stakeholder Engagement**

Sally was having a hard time picking out the features for her shower. "Rick, you've done a lot of bathrooms what do you think I should pick?" **(Interview)**

Rick put his hands up with his palms facing out. "I just order what I'm told. I'm not any good with the design stuff, but I *can* tell you once you pick something out if it is going to work with the project. You should ask your friends!"

The Next Evening

"OK, ladies! Thanks for coming over tonight!" Sally smiled at her friends sitting around her family room. "I need your help figuring out what to put in my new shower. You wouldn't think this would be so hard, but I'm doubting myself because I seem to like everything!"

Her friend Melissa laughed.

"There *are* lots of choices! So, what is your priority? Personal style or resale value?"

"That's a great question!" Sally said. "A little of both. I want to love it but I have to take into account how a buyer might see it. That's why I need you guys!" **(Focus Group)** "I downloaded a checklist from one of those home improvement websites, and it says I should have been making these decisions a while ago!" **(Checklist)**

Using her computer Sally projected the screen's image onto the TV so that everyone could see. "I was thinking we could flip through the pictures on this design website to get ideas and save the ones we like to my computer. Are you ready?" **(Brainstorm)**

Decision Making

Used 13 Times!

<u>Definition:</u> **The act or process of deciding something especially with a group of people**

<u>When/Where:</u> **Monitor and Control Project Work, Perform Integrated Change Control, Collect Requirements, Define Scope, Validate Scope, Estimate Costs, Plan Quality Management, Manage Quality, Acquire Resources, Plan Risk Responses, Plan Stakeholder Engagement, Monitor Stakeholder Engagement**

Sally couldn't help but laugh out loud as she listened to her friends discuss the different choices for the bathroom.

"You are worse than I am! We've gone through so many pictures! I think we've got enough to take a vote." **(Voting)**

Sally put an image of each design choice on the TV, and had her friends raise their hands to vote for their favorite. "Well, at least I can say that my friends are individuals! You don't agree on any of the choices! Well, except for Rachel and Melissa. They were the only two out of all of you that agreed on any one of them! **(Plurality)** I think the only thing we all agreed on tonight was ordering pizza!! **(Unanimity)** She laughed.

"I think that's enough for the night! Let's watch a movie!" **(Autocratic)**

PMIS

Used 12 Times!

Definition: **A part of the environmental factors, providing access to tools, such as a scheduling tool, a work authorization system, a configuration management system, an information collection and distribution system, or interfaces to other online automated systems. Automated gathering and reporting on key performance indicators (KPI) can be part of this system.**

When/Where: **Direct and Manage Project Work, Sequence Activities, Develop Schedule, Control Schedule, Estimate Costs, Control Costs, Estimate Activity Resources, Manage Team, Control Resources, Manage Communications, Monitor Communications, Implement Risk Responses**

"Hey! What happened to your magic binder?" Angela asked Sally when they met for lunch. Sally laughed.

"I got tired of lugging the whole thing around. I decided to put it all on my iPad using an organizational App. Makes it a lot easier when I need to send something to Rick."

"But it doesn't have all your cute tabs to track everything," Angela teased.

"Ah ha! But it does." Sally opened up the program to show her friend. "See, it divides everything into files so that I know who's doing what and when. Rick even can access it to update it. I like to know who's in the house, so either he can update the program or send me a text and I'll input it." **(Worker Authorization)**

"I should have known you'd find an even more efficient way of keeping tabs on everything!" Sally was too busy shutting down her iPad to notice Angela's sarcastic tone.

Data Representation

Used 11 Times!

Definition: **Information that is communicated verbally or stored and distributed in various formats as reports**

When/Where: **Collect Requirements, Plan Quality Management, Manage Quality, Control Quality, Plan Resource Management, Plan Communications Management, Monitor Communications, Perform Qualitative Analysis, Identify Stakeholders, Plan Stakeholder Engagement, Monitor Stakeholder Engagement**

"Where did the white board come from?" Ben asked Sally when he got home from work.

"I picked it up at the store on the way home. It seemed like a great way of keeping track." Ben read the list on the whiteboard out loud. " 'Slick look tile, modern faucet' Are these ideas or what you have chosen?"**(Mind Mapping)**

"Just some ideas. I'm trying to group together the different elements that I like, so I can see them all in one place."

"Huh! That's not a bad idea," Ben said turning towards her.

"Well, if you like the white board, you are going to *love* my Pinterest page!" Sally exclaimed.

"What the heck is a Pinterest?" Ben looked bewildered as Sally opened her iPad and brought up the website.

"It's a virtual bulletin board, look..." She turned the iPad so that he could see the screen. "You search the web for inspiration and click on the pictures that you want to remember." The screen was covered in folders with headers labeled 'faucet', 'tile', 'funny' etc. She clicked on the file labeled faucets, which opened up several pictures of different types of faucets. "See, I've saved all the faucets that I found online that I thought would work!"

Ben flipped through the different pictures before chuckling.

“What?” Sally asked.

“Well, on your white board you have ‘modern faucet’, but most of the pictures you’ve chosen on here are traditional in style.”

Sally bent her head closer to look.

“You’re right! I guess I like traditional too.” She wrinkled her nose. “I think the modern faucets will work better with the whole design, but I want to hang on to the others in case we use them in the future. Here,” swiftly, using the keyboard, she created a new file titled ‘traditional faucet’ and retitled the first folder ‘modern faucet’. Using her mouse, she separated the pictures into the two different categories. **(Affinity Diagrams)**

“So what did you put under ‘funny’?” Ben asked when she was done. Sally blushed.

“Hey!” Ben laughed as she opened the folder to show him. “Some of those construction memes are actually pretty funny!”

OUTPUTS

Project Document Updates

Used 39 Times!

Definition: **Any change to a controlled or noncontrolled document related to the project.**

When/Where: **Direct and Manage Project Work, Monitor and Control Project Work, Perform Integrated Change Controls, Close Project or Phase, Define Scope, Create WBS, Validate Scope, Control Scope, Sequence Activities, Estimate Activity Durations, Develop Schedule, Control Schedule, Estimate Costs, Determine Budget, Control Costs, Plan Quality Management, Manage Quality, Control Quality, Plan Resource Management, Estimate Activity Resources, Acquire Resources, Develop Team, Manage Team, Control Resources, Plan Communications Management, Manage Communications, Monitor Communications, Identify Risks, Perform Qualitative Analysis, Perform Quantitative Analysis, Plan Risk Responses, Implement Risk Responses, Monitor Risks, Plan Procurement Management, Conduct Procurements, Control Procurements, Identify Stakeholders, Manage Stakeholder Engagement, Monitor Stakeholder Engagement,**

Rick was waiting for Sally when she got home one afternoon towards the end of the project. Warily, she got out of the car.

"Should I be worried that you are waiting for me?" she asked only half joking.

"Not worried exactly, but definitely something we need to talk about." He put his hands up in defense. "Remember, don't shoot the messenger!"

"Now you *are* worrying me!!"

"Apparently, my normal building inspector has broken his leg and is out on leave." He looked at his clipboard. "Our new inspector is Larry Miller." He made a face. "According to my buddy at the City, Larry is pretty tough."

Sally frowned. "But surely whatever you're doing is up to code.....right?"

“Oh absolutely” Rick assured her. “It’s just that some inspectors nit-pick or are slow to come out. I like working with the other guy because I know what to expect.”

“Larry Miller, you said? I’ll add his name to the contact list and take out the old inspector’s name. **(Update Stakeholder Register)** I guess I need to make time to meet this guy too.**(Update Activity List)**” She sighed. “Do you think we should worry about him?”

“To be honest, if he’s as tough as they say he is, it might set us back some time in the schedule.” **(Update Risk Register)**

“Greeeaaaattt!” Sally moaned.

PMP Updates

Used 26 Times!

Definition: **Changes to the Project Management Plan throughout the course of the project**

When/Where: **Direct and Manage Project Work, Manage Project Knowledge, Monitor and Control Project Work, Perform Integrated Change Controls, Control Scope, Define Activities, Develop Schedule, Control Schedule, Control Costs, Plan Quality Management, Manage Quality, Control Quality, Acquire Resources, Develop Team, Manage Team, Control Resources, Plan Communications Plan, Plan Communications Management, Manage Communications, Monitor Communications, Plan Risk Responses, Monitor Risks, Conduct Procurements, Control Procurements, Identify Stakeholders, Manage Stakeholder Engagement**

"How married is your husband to the idea of a Japanese toilet?" Rick asked.

"Why?" Sally dreaded the answer. *Please don't let there be another problem!!*

"I just saw a German toilet at a trade show and it has basically all the same features of the Japanese one, but..." Rick grinned. "Not only is it cheaper, a store in town stocks them so we can eliminate the two weeks we were going to have to wait for the other one to ship!"

Sally grinned! "That sounds perfect! Let's do that! I doubt Ben will even notice the difference!"

Two days later......

"Sally!" Ben yelled for his wife from the bathroom under construction.

"What?" She asked joining him.

"What is this toilet? This isn't the one I picked out! This has German writing all over the box!"

"Are you sure that's not Japanese?" Sally teased. Ben glared, unamused by her joke.

"What's going on Sally?"

"Hang on, let me get my iPad and I'll show you why I decided to go with this one."

Opening up her project App on her iPad, she showed him the file with the Risk Baseline. "See this is where our risk was." She pointed at the line. "Now here is what our actual risk is." She pointed at a dot lower on the graph. **(Update Risk Baseline)** "Rick found it at a trade show and the local store had it in stock so it minimized our risk. Now even better than that....look at these two." She opened two windows so that she could show him that on the cost and schedule graphs the actual data dots were significantly lower than the original baselines. **(Update Schedule Baseline, Update Cost Baseline)** "It's essentially the same toilet just made by a German company."

"Wow! That really saved us some time and money, huh?" Ben shrugged. "It's just a toilet I guess. I'd rather save the money than have it speak Japanese to me!"

Change Requests

Used 24 times!

Definition: **Any written request that is submitted to whatever change control board or decision making group has been implemented.**

When/Where: **Bid Documents, Change Requests, Closed Procurements, Communications Management Plan, Cost Baseline, Cost Estimates, Cost Forecasts, Cost Management Plan, Deliverables, Duration Estimates, EEF Updates, Final Product, Service or Result Transition, Final Report, Independent Cost Estimates, Issue Log, Lessons Learned Register, Make or Buy Decisions, Milestone List, OPA Updates**

"What's this?" Sally asked as Rick shoved a shower enclosure brochure into her hand.

"This is something else I found at the trade show. Since you were happy about the toilet, I thought I'd show you this too." He pointed to the picture. "I know you wanted a regular frameless glass enclosure but this one has a modern wave on the edge that I think would look really cool in your bathroom!"

"Is this the same thing as before? Less time and money?"

Rick grimaced. "Unfortunately, no. The local glass guy has it in stock but I think it is going to be a little more than the original one you picked out."

"It *is* really cool looking! Can you write up what the difference would be in terms of cost and schedule? I'll show it to Ben and let you know. **(Change Request)** Thanks for keeping your eye out! We really appreciate it!"

Work Performance Information

Used 10 times!

Definition: **The performance data collected from various controlling processes, analyzed in context and integrated based on relationships across areas.**

When/Where: **Validate Scope, Control Scope, Control Schedule, Control Costs, Control Quality, Control Resources, Monitor Communications, Monitor Risks, Control Procurements, Monitor Stakeholder Engagement**

"I just looked at the bathroom and the shower looks great! Almost done right?" Ben asked as he came in the room. "Dare I ask how we are doing on the overall budget? I know that we've had some changes along the way…". Sally smiled, she'd been anticipating this conversation.

"Here, let me show you what I've got." Sally turned her iPad towards her husband so that he could better see the graph. "I took all the raw data that was coming in, in the form of actual money going out, and analyzed it so that it created an easy to read graph!" **(WPI)**

"So, the line is where you thought we'd be originally, and the dots that make up the second line show what we've actually spent?" He asked.

"Yup! As you can see, we are actually under budget!" Sally crowed.

"You're right, that is easy to understand. I can see that we are $25 under budget. I'm not sure that amount is worthy of the enthusiasm you're giving it, but it's great that we aren't *over* budget! Good work keeping track of all this."

Organizational Process Updates

Used 9 times!

Definition: **Updates to the plans, processes, policies, procedures, and knowledge bases specific to and used by the performing organization.**

When/Where: **Resource Breakdown Structure, Resource Calendars, Resource Management Plan, Resource Requirements, Risk Management Plan, Risk Register, Risk Report, Schedule Baseline**

Setting down her iPad, Sally looked thoughtful.

"Ben, you know how we used the schedule template from the floors to come up with the schedule for the bathroom?"

"Yes..." He answered warily.

"Well I was just thinking that during this bathroom project we've had to change the schedule some. It was a bigger project with more moving parts than the floors. I think when we do the next bathroom project, I'll be able to use this improved schedule template to give us a more accurate idea of how long a remodel will take." **(Organizational Process Asset Update**)

"*What next bathroom project???*"

Basis of Estimates

Used 3 times!

***<u>Definition</u>:* Information that goes into cost, schedule and resources.**

***<u>When/Where</u>:* Agreements, Approved Change Requests, Assumption Log**

A Few Months Earlier……

Sally and Ben were sitting at the kitchen table going over their contractor Rick's proposed estimate for the remodel of their Master Bath.

"It looks reasonable." Sally said hopefully.

"It's definitely in the ballpark of what I was thinking, but do you know how he came up with his estimate? I mean is he just guessing? I don't want a ton of change orders that brings the price up down the line," Ben said.

"I talked to Rick about it before he wrote it up. He's done a bunch of bathroom remodels before. He said that what we want done to our shower is very similar to a house he did last year. I think he is basing it off his previous experience." **(Basis of Estimate)** "Also, I gave him the general style of tile I want so he was able to give me an estimate of the tile cost as long as I stick to that price grade." **(Basis of Estimate)**

"Are you sure you're ready to be without your shower for the next several months?" Ben asked seriously.

"Absolutely! I'm so excited for the project to get started."

"In that case, I guess you should give Rick the green light."

EEF Updates

Used 3 Times!

Definition: **Updates to the Enterprise Environmental Factors.**

When/Where: **Project Schedule Network Diagrams, Project Scope Statement, Project Team Assignments**

"Oh my gosh! Who's this cute little guy?" Rick asked as the black and white bundle of fur barreled up to him yipping. Sally scooped up the puppy.

"This is Oreo! He's the newest addition to the household." Rick ruffled the puppy's fur.

"He's adorable!"

"He'll be in the laundry room behind the baby gate while I'm at work, but he's started jumping; and the bigger he gets, the more I worry he'll eventually clear that fence. I hate to ask, but could you just be sure that you are closing the door when you are carrying things in and out?"

"Sure, that's not a problem." Mentally Rick was wondering if he'd be listening to a bored puppy bark all day! **(Enterprise Environmental Factors Updates)** "I'll also be sure that we are extra careful cleaning up at the end of the day. Puppies will eat anything!"

"Thank you so much, Rick! I really appreciate it.

ADDITIONAL TERMS

INPUTS

Agreements: Any document or communication that defines the initial intentions of a project. This can take the form of a contract, memorandum of understanding (MOU), letters of agreement, verbal agreements, email, etc.

Business Documents: Comprised of the Project Business Case and the Project Benefits Management Plan.

Procurement Documentation: All documents used in signing, executing, and closing an agreement. Procurement documentation may include documents predating the project.

Work Performance Reports(WPR): The physical or electronic representation of work performance information compiled in project documents, intended to generate decisions, actions, or awareness.

Approved Change Requests: A part of change control where a change within a project is approved.

Deliverables: Any unique and verifiable product, result, or capability to perform a service that is required to be produced to complete a process, phase, or project.

Change Requests: A formal proposal to modify a document, deliverable, or baseline.

Outputs from Other Processes: A product, result, or service generated by a process. May be an input to a successor process.

Project Funding Requirements: Forecast project costs to be paid that are derived from the cost baseline for total or periodic requirements, including projected expenditures plus anticipated liabilities.

Seller Proposals: Formal responses from sellers to a request for proposal or other procurement document specifying the price, commercial terms of sale, and technical specifications or capabilities the seller will do for the requesting organization that, if accepted, would bind the seller to perform the resulting agreement.

Team Performance Assessments: The evaluation of a team's effectiveness that may include indicators such as: *Improvements in skills* *that allow individuals to perform assignments more effectively, Improvements in competencies that help team members perform better as a team, Reduced staff turnover rate, and Increased team cohesiveness where team members share information and experiences openly and help each other to improve the overall project performance.*

Verified Deliverables: Completed project deliverables that have been checked and confirmed for correctness through the Control Quality process.

TOOLS

Analogous Estimating: A technique for estimating the duration or cost of an activity or a project using historical data from a similar activity or project.

Audits: These are of the process not the product. An audit is a structured, independent process used to determine if project activities comply with organizational and project policies, processes, and procedures. Identifying all good and best practices being implemented; Identifying all nonconformity, gaps, and shortcomings; Sharing good practices introduced or implemented in similar projects in the organization and/or industry; Proactively offering assistance in a positive manner to improve the implementation of processes to help raise team productivity; and Highlighting contributions of each audit in the lessons learned repository of the organization.

Bottom-Up Estimating: A method of estimating project duration or cost by aggregating the estimates of the lower-level components of the work breakdown structure (WBS).

Communication Skills: Techniques that include *Communication Competence* (clarity of purpose in key messages, effective relationships and information sharing, leadership behaviors), *Feedback* (coaching, mentoring, negotiating), *Nonverbal* (gestures, tone of voice, mirroring, eye contact Etc.) and *Presentations* (progress reports, background information, general information, objectives) for the purpose of conveying pertinent information for the success of the project.

Communication Technology: Specific tools, systems, computer programs, etc. used to transfer information among project stakeholders.

Inspection: Examination of a work product to determine whether it conforms to documented standards.

Leads and Lags: The amount of time whereby a successor activity can be advanced with respect to a predecessor activity and the amount of time whereby a successor activity will be delayed with respect to a predecessor activity.

Parametric Estimating: An estimating technique in which an algorithm is used to calculate cost or duration based on historical data and project parameters.

Communication Methods:

Interactive communication: Between two or more parties performing a multidirectional exchange of information in real time. It employs communications artifacts such as meetings, phone calls, instant messaging, some forms of social media, and videoconferencing.

Push communication: Sent or distributed directly to specific recipients who need to receive the information. This ensures that the information is distributed but does not ensure that it actually reached or was understood by the intended audience. Push communications artifacts include letters, memos, reports, emails, faxes, voice mails, blogs, and press releases.

Pull communication: Used for large complex information sets, or for large audiences, and requires the recipients to access content at their own discretion subject to security procedures. These methods include web portals, intranet sites, e-learning, lessons learned databases, or knowledge repositories.

Critical Path Method(CPM): A method used to estimate the minimum project duration and determine the amount of schedule flexibility on the logical network paths within the schedule model.

Decomposition: A technique used for dividing and subdividing the project scope and project deliverables into smaller, more manageable parts.

Problem Solving: A search for solutions for issues or challenges. It can include gathering additional information, critical thinking, creative, quantitative and/or logical approaches. Methods include: *Defining the problem, Identifying the root-cause, Generating possible solutions, Choosing the best solution, Implementing the solution, and Verifying solution effectiveness.*

Resource Optimization: A technique in which activity start and finish dates are adjusted to balance demand for resources with the available supply.

Schedule Compression: A technique used to shorten the schedule duration without reducing the project scope.

Three-Point Estimating: A technique used to estimate cost or duration by applying an average or weighted average of optimistic, pessimistic, and most likely estimates when there is uncertainty with the individual activity estimates.

Virtual Teams: Groups of people with a shared goal who fulfill their roles with little or no time spent meeting face to face.

Outputs

Accepted Deliverables: Products, results, or capabilities produced by a project and validated by the project customer or sponsors as meeting their specified acceptance criteria.

Activity Attributes: Multiple attributes associated with each schedule activity that can be included within the activity list. Activity attributes include activity codes, predecessor activities, successor activities, logical relationships, leads and lags, resource requirements, imposed dates, constraints, and assumptions.

Activity List: A documented tabulation of schedule activities that shows the activity description, activity identifier, and a sufficiently detailed scope of work description so project team members understand what work is to be performed.

Agreements: Any document or communication that defines the initial intentions of a project. This can take the form of a contract, memorandum of understanding (MOU), letters of agreement, verbal agreements, email, etc.

Approved Change Requests: A part of change control where a change within a project is approved.

Assumption Log: A project document used to record all assumptions and constraints throughout the project life cycle.

Bid Documents: All documents used to solicit information, quotations, or proposals from prospective sellers.

Closed Procurements: Formal approval that a project has been either terminated or completed.

Communications Management Plan: A component of the project management plan that describes how to identify and account for project artifacts under configuration control, and how to record and report changes to them.

Cost Baseline: The approved version of the time-phased project budget, excluding any management reserves, which can be changed only through formal change control procedures and is used as a basis for comparison to actual results.

Cost Estimates: An approximation of the monetary resources needed to complete project activities.

Cost Forecasts: The process of developing the future trends along with the assessment of probabilities, uncertainties and inflation that could occur during the project.

Cost Management Plan: A component of a project or program management plan that describes how costs will be planned, structured, and controlled.

Deliverables: Any unique and verifiable product, result, or capability to perform a service that is required to be produced to complete a process, phase, or project.

Duration Estimates: A quantitative assessment of the likely amount of the total number of work periods required to complete an activity or work breakdown structure component, expressed in hours, days, or weeks. Contrast with effort.

Final Product, Service or Result Transition: A product, service, or result, once delivered by the project, may be handed over to a different group or organization that will operate, maintain, and support it throughout its life cycle. This output refers to the transition of the final product, service, or result that the project was authorized to produce (or in the case of phase closure, the intermediate product, service, or result of that phase) from one team to another.

Final Report: Provides a summary of the project performance. It can include information such as:

- Summary level descriptions of the project or phase
- Scope objectives, the criteria used to evaluate the scope, and evidence that the completion criteria were met

• Quality objectives, the criteria used to evaluate the project and product quality, the verification and actual milestone delivery dates, and reasons for variances

• Cost objectives, including the acceptable cost range, actual costs, and reasons for any variances

• Summary of the validation information for the final product, service, or result

• Schedule objectives, including whether results achieved the benefits that the project was undertaken to address. If the benefits are not met at the close of the project, indicate the degree to which they were achieved and estimate for future benefits realization

• Summary of how the final product, service, or result achieved the business needs identified in the business plan. If the business needs are not met at the close of the project, indicate the degree to which they were achieved and estimate for when the business needs will be met in the future

• Summary of any risks or issues encountered on the project and how they were addressed

Independent Cost Estimates: A process that uses a third party to collect as well as analyze information that is then used to predict cost.

Issue Log: A project document where information about issues is recorded and monitored

Lessons Learned Register: A project document used to record knowledge gained during a project so that it can be used in the current project and entered into the lessons learned repository.

Make or Buy Decisions: Decisions made regarding the external purchase or internal manufacture of a product.

Milestone List: A list of significant points or events in a project, program, or portfolio.

Physical Resource Assignments: Record of the material, equipment, supplies, locations, and other physical resources that will be used during the project.

Procurement Documentation Updates: Updates to the documents utilized in bid and proposal activities, which include the buyer's Invitation for bid, invitation for negotiations, request for information, request for quotation, request for proposal, and seller's responses.

Procurement Management Plan: A component of the project or program management plan that describes how a project team will acquire goods and services from outside of the performing organization.

Procurement Statement of Work: Description of the procurement item in sufficient detail to allow prospective sellers to determine if they are capable of providing the products, services, or results.

Procurement Strategy: The approach by the buyer to determine the project delivery method and the type of legally binding agreement(s) that should be used to deliver the desired results.

Project Calendars: A calendar that identifies working days and shifts that are available for scheduled activities.

Project Charter: A document issued by the project initiator or sponsor that formally authorizes the existence of a project and provides the project manager with the authority to apply organizational resources to project activities.

Project Communications: Project Communications Management includes the processes required to ensure timely and appropriate planning, collection, creation, distribution, storage, retrieval, management, control, monitoring, and ultimate disposition of project information.

Project Funding Requirements: Forecast of project costs to be paid that are derived from the cost baseline for total or periodic requirements, including projected expenditures plus anticipated liabilities

Project Schedule: A listing of a project's milestones, activities, and deliverables, usually with intended start and finish dates

Project Schedule Network Diagrams: A graphical representation of the logical relationships among the project schedule activities.

Project Scope Statement: The description of the project scope, major deliverables, assumptions, and constraints.

Project Team Assignments: Record of the team members and their roles and responsibilities for the project. Documentation can include: *project team directory and names inserted into the project management plan, such as the project organization charts and schedules.*

Quality Control Measurements: The documented results of control quality activities.

Quality Management Plan: A component of the project or program management plan that describes how applicable policies, procedures, and guidelines will be implemented to achieve the quality objectives.

Quality Metrics: A description of a project or product attribute and how to measure it.

Quality Reports: A project document that includes quality management issues, recommendations for corrective actions, and a summary of findings from quality control activities and may include recommendations for process, project, and product improvements.

Requirements Documentation: A description of how individual requirements meet the business need for the project

Requirements Management Plan: A component of the project or program management plan that describes how requirements will be analyzed, documented, and managed.

Requirements Traceability Matrix: A grid that links product requirements from their origin to the deliverables that satisfy them.

Resource Breakdown Structure: A hierarchical representation of resources by category and type.

Resource Calendars: A calendar that identifies the working days and shifts upon which each specific resource is available.

Resource Management Plan: A component of the project management plan that describes how project resources are acquired, allocated, monitored, and controlled.

Resource Requirements: The types and quantities of resources required for each activity in a work package.

Risk Management Plan: A component of the project, program, or portfolio management plan that describes how risk management activities will be structured and performed.

Risk Register: A repository in which outputs of risk management processes are recorded.

Risk Report: A project document developed progressively throughout the Project Risk Management processes, which summarizes information on individual project risks and the level of overall project risk.

Schedule Baseline: The approved version of a schedule model that can be changed using formal change control procedures and is used as the basis for comparison to actual results.

Schedule Data: The collection of information for describing and controlling the schedule.

Schedule Forecasts: Estimates or predictions of conditions and events in the project's future based on information and knowledge available at the time the schedule is calculated.

Schedule Management Plan: A component of the project or program management plan that establishes the criteria and the activities for developing, monitoring, and controlling the schedule.

Scope Baseline: The approved version of a scope statement, work breakdown structure (WBS), and its associated WBS dictionary, that can be changed using formal change control procedures and is used as a basis for comparison to actual results.

Scope Management Plan: A component of the project or program management plan that describes how the scope will be defined, developed, monitored, controlled, and validated.

Selected Sellers: A provider or supplier of products, services, or results to an organization

Source Selection Criteria: A set of attributes desired by the buyer which a seller is required to meet or exceed to be selected for a contract.

Stakeholder Engagement Plan: A component of the project management plan that identifies the strategies and actions required to promote productive involvement of stakeholders in project or program decision making and execution.

Stakeholder Register: A project document including the identification, assessment, and classification of project stakeholders.

Team Charter: A document that records the team values, agreements, and operating guidelines, as well as establishing clear expectations regarding acceptable behavior by project team members.

Team Performance Assessments: Formal or informal assessments of the project team's effectiveness as the project progresses

Test and Evaluation Documents: Project documents that describe the activities used to determine if the product meets the quality objectives stated in the quality management plan.

Verified Deliverables: Completed project deliverables that have been checked and confirmed for correctness through the Control Quality process.

Work Performance Reports(WPR): The physical or electronic representation of work performance information compiled in project documents, intended to generate decisions, actions, or awareness

ABOUT THE AUTHORS

Kate Breitfeller is the President of BreitIdeas Inc, a Global Training and Consulting Corporation. Founded in 2005, BreitIdeas has grown from a small Business Consulting firm to a globally positioned corporation with clients ranging from Fortune 100 Corporations to Small Startups looking for guidance.

Jason Breitfeller, MBA, PMP is an International Consultant, Trainer and Coach. With over 20 years of experience in project management, Jason has successfully trained thousands of PMPs and has successfully worked with companies such as Siemens, NorthropGrumman, Airbus, and Harris Corporation.

www.ingramcontent.com/pod-product-compliance
Lightning Source LLC
Chambersburg PA
CBHW070516220526
45467CB00002B/687
* 9 7 8 1 7 1 7 3 9 6 9 3 8 *